How to Get an Acting Job outside of New York and Hollywood!

Terry Harris

You can visit Terry's website at www.terryharris.tv.

National Library of Canada Cataloguing in Publication

Harris, Terry
        How to get an acting job outside of New York and
Hollywood! / Terry Harris.

ISBN 1-4120-0327-X

        1. Acting—Vocational guidance.   I. Title.

PN2055.H37 2003   792'.028'023   C2003-902581-0

TRAFFORD

This book was published on-demand in cooperation with Trafford Publishing.
On-demand publishing is a unique process and service of making a book available for
retail sale to the public taking advantage of on-demand manufacturing and Internet
marketing. **On-demand publishing** includes promotions, retail sales, manufacturing, order
fulfilment, accounting and collecting royalties on behalf of the author.

Suite 6E, 2333 Government St., Victoria, B.C. V8T 4P4, CANADA

Phone	250-383-6864	Toll-free	1-888-232-4444 (Canada & US)
Fax	250-383-6804	E-mail	sales@trafford.com
Web site	www.trafford.com	TRAFFORD PUBLISHING IS A DIVISION OF TRAFFORD HOLD-	

INGS LTD.

Trafford Catalogue #03-0696   www.trafford.com/robots/03-0696.html

10   9   8   7   6   5   4   3   2

Contents

Chapters:

DEDICATION

This book is lovingly dedicated to my father, the late George A. Harris, and my stepmother, the late Dolores Sebeck Harris. I don't know how to thank you for the legacy of love and the many material and spiritual gifts you have bequeathed me throughout my life. May you know only peace, love, and purpose in the spiritual realm. I miss your laughter and your love and affection. From the depths of my heart, thank you for the many blessings you lovingly bestowed upon me. This book is for you.

Love,
Terry

INTRODUCTION

Drama is one of the most creative and compelling art forms the world has ever known. Acting is truly one of the most artistically fulfilling and creatively satisfying activities an individual can experience. *How to Get an Acting Job Outside of New York and Hollywood* is a book that serves as a creative and practical manual for aspiring actors, drama teachers, directors, and students of theatre unable to move to the major markets, but who seek an outlet for their creative talents. This book examines and explores a multitude of opportunities for actors and performing artists outside of the major markets of New York and Hollywood. An authentic aspiration of this book is to help actors find creative and artistic satisfaction wherever they live and work. Professional educators, directors, actors, producers, photographers, videographers, and theatre artists share valuable information and insights.

One of the most difficult decisions for actors and performing artists to make has always been where to move to find acting and performing opportunities. Do you really have to move to New York or Hollywood to find creative satisfaction and opportunities as an actor? Do you really have to leave your family, friends, and geographic region to work as an actor, performing artist, or print model?

If fame and fortune is your goal, then the answer is probably yes. However, if creative expression, artistic fulfillment, and theatrical satisfaction is your goal, then the answer is no. There are numerous acting, performing, and modeling opportunities all over this immense country. This book will explore acting, performing, and modeling opportunities outside of those traditional markets previously mentioned. In this book, you will learn how to tap into the markets for nonunion acting work in theatre, TV commercials, corporate videos, and commercial print modeling. Another objective of this book is to aid you in creating your own theatrical and artistic experiences on stage and in front of the camera.

The ultimate goal of this book is to help you realize that you can create viable, dynamic, artistic experiences in your own "neck of the woods." Creativity knows no limits, and this book will aid you in exploring imaginative alternatives to working and struggling in the major markets. Is this possible? Can you perform and make money at your art outside of the "Big Leagues" of New York and Hollywood? Well, in a very real sense I am a perfect example of how it can indeed be done: as an actor, I have performed in over 35 plays, 50 TV commercials, 30 corporate videos, and 250 modeling jobs. I have hosted several TV shows, infomercials, and nationally distributed videos. I have appeared in national print ads, regional brochures, national travel guidebooks, and on state billboards. I have taught drama at the college level, and have conducted numerous theatre and drama workshops at respected art institutions on the East Coast. In these pages, I will share with you the necessary insights into launching a career from your own geographic area. You can create your own theatrical and performing experiences in imaginative and artistically compelling ways. So, read on, and realize that your creative and artistic fate is truly in your own hands...

CHAPTER ONE
BEGIN IT NOW!

"Whatever you do, or dream you can do, begin it. Genius has magic, power, and boldness in it. Begin it now."

Goethe, German playwright, poet, and director (1749-1832)

The word theatre comes for the ancient Greek word Theatron - the "seeing place." When Drama evolved over two thousand years ago during the Golden Age of Greece, the citizens of the time would travel to the week long Festival of Dionysus to experience the Drama - "the action" - which was held at the Theatron - "the seeing place." The inherent power of theatre since its origins in ancient Greece has been to spiritually and aesthetically uplift and move an audience through its drama (actions). Catharsis was the aim and ideal of classical Greek drama, and the Greek playwrights aspired to spiritually purge the audience through their compelling and dramatic works.

During the early twentieth century, the French theorist Antonin Artaud believed that theatre could be a truly dynamic, imaginative, exciting, and creative experience. Indeed, Artaud was committed to a bold, new vision of drama. He aspired to create a theatre that was meaningful and vital for the modern world. Artaud offered many unique and innovative ideas in the realm of acting and theatre - specifically, he believed that acting spaces and acting areas could include such places as barns, vacant airplane hangers, and single rooms. Artaud's revolutionary ideas about what theatre could be gave rise to authentic innovation in modern theatre. Today, theatre practitioners can create new visions and vistas for theatre in our modern ever-changing world, due to the innovative ideas and ideals of theatre theoreticians like Artaud. Indeed, a creative vision of the theatre is needed in the modern world, if this remarkable art form is to flourish in the centuries to come.

How to Get an Acting Job Outside of New York and Hollywood is an artistic guidebook that will explore a rich variety of creative and imaginative ways of producing viable, artistic, and theatrical experiences for today and tomorrow. This book will explore a multitude of multimedia acting opportunities for actors and performing artists outside of the major markets of New York and Hollywood. Another aspiration of this book is to help actors and performing artists find creative and artistic satisfaction wherever they live and work.

Since theatrical experiences can occur and be seen at any place and time, the only limitations are those that a performing artist places on himself. From the classical amphitheatres of ancient Greece and Rome, to the medieval pageant wagons of Western Europe, or the stages of the Renaissance, theatre occurs when the drama is heard and seen by an audience that seeks spiritual and artistic enlightenment. Theatre, then, can occur in barns, catwalks, or the corners of a room, as Artaud suggested. Theatre, with its wealth of artistic possibilities, has no creative limits. As we enter the twenty-first century, with the rich promise of a Renaissance in the arts, we must rise to the creative challenge of producing a vibrant and meaningful theatre. And we must realize that theatre can encompass a rich variety of multimedia acting experiences. It is imperative that we reach out to the young through the theatre as well, and inspire them to take the artistic torch, if this compelling and emotionally evocative art form is to flourish into the future.

The promise of theatre is the very promise of our cultural legacy. Theatre has always been artistically, intellectually, and culturally intertwined with the society from which it has emerged. Theatre has reflected the ideals, ideas, dreams, and hopes of its society. Theatre has shown us not only who we are, but who we might become as human beings.

Theatre and the dramatic arts have shown us a glimpse of our very humanity - a glimpse of our most noble deeds and our most wretched acts. Theatre has explored the human soul like no other art form, exhibiting to us the colors of our very characters, casting a klieg light on our virtues and foibles as human beings, always within the artistic structure of tragedy and comedy.

The creative imagination of the theatre practitioner is paramount to the ultimate success of this future theatre. The human imagination - that is, the image-making machine of the mind's eye - has been an integral element for the theatre's artistic success through the ages.

The human imagination is, after all, the authentic creative vision of the artist. Throughout the history of the theatre, different acting styles have flourished, all with varying degrees of creative bravado and artistic success. From the robust acting skills and styles of the Commedia Dell'arte to the bold confrontational acting styles of the modern theatre, the creative styles and techniques of a particular time and era have always fulfilled their theatre's aesthetic and artistic needs.

A creative vision of the theatre of the future is truly needed. The theatre artist must explore a rich variety of ways to present theatre to a modern audience. If the theatre is to remain an essential cultural element in our society, as it has throughout history, then the theatre artist must make theatre creatively relevant to our time.

The theatre artist must learn to produce theatre in new and unique ways. Art and technology must merge in a creatively practical and aesthetically pleasing manner for this new, bold theatre of the future. The theatre artist must explore imaginative and innovative ways to entertain and emotionally touch audiences, bringing them to the full power and promise of the theatrical experience. Creative and unconventional approaches to the execution and presentation of theatre must be considered. A creative vision has to take hold of the theatre artist, and this vision must be fully realized and imaginatively implemented.

The theorist and director Jerzy Grotowski believed that a "holy" actor in a "poor" theatre was needed to fulfill theatre's promise and destiny. Grotowski imagined and created a theatre devoid of excessive props and scenery (a poor theatre) and actors devoid of excessive costumes and make-up (the holy actor) in order for theatre to approach an almost spiritual experience. Since drama and religion seemed to have evolved from the same spiritual impulse, Grotowski's ideas are profound. As technology advances and flourishes in the twenty-first century, audiences will actively seek an artist's creative vision of the human condition. Intrinsic to all theatre, from the beginning of time, is the full exploration of the human being and the human psyche. For the human condition - the human experience - transcends time and space.

What makes the great Greek tragedy, *Oedipus the King* by Sophocles, a classic, is the playwright's understanding of human nature, and his ability to theatrically present Oedipus' tragedy in a way that touches us even today.

When Shakespeare wrote *Hamlet*, he created a poignant and complex character that we recognize in ourselves, and thus Shakespeare's drama transcends time and teaches us a profound lesson about the human condition. *Hamlet* reverberates in our consciousness to this day because it touches the deepest core of the human dilemma. We recognize Hamlet's angst, and we empathize with this most universal, and at times, most misunderstood of characters. The classics are classics because they reach beyond the centuries through their sheer dramatic power and theatricality to share their understanding and comprehension of human nature and the human experience. Remember that

Sophocles and Shakespeare were men of the theatre, they were actors, writers, and occasional directors.

Sophocles and Shakespeare knew how to sculpt their words for dramatic impact so that their dramas reverberated in our minds *and* our hearts. Both men had a creative vision of their respective theatres. Sophocles is credited with the addition of scene painting to the Greek theatre, fixing the chorus at 15, and introducing the third actor to drama. Shakespeare was a theatrical innovator as well as a creative wordsmith and Renaissance man of the theatre. Shakespeare advanced the drama to a new level of artistic excellence during the Elizabethan Renaissance. Both artists had a vision of what theatre could be, and they employed their raw talents and imaginations to create a theatre of their time that deeply moved their audiences.

A creative vision, then, is intrinsic to the development and nurturing of the theatre. Creativity celebrates the profound question, "what if." When the Russian director Constantin Stanislavsky created the concept of "The Magic If," he unleashed a torrent of creative thoughts, ideas, and feelings that led to modern acting theory. Stanislavsky realized that, "The Magic If" would serve as a creative impetus to the human imagination. What would you do *if* you came home from college, and your father had died mysteriously, and your mother had married your uncle? An actor playing *Hamlet* would employ "The Magic If" to stimulate his creative imagination and become engaged in the given circumstances of Hamlet's tragic situation. As an actor, director, and drama teacher, Stanislavsky realized that actors need "The Magic If" to propel their minds and feelings into a creative realm of character identification. The actors can then give a truthful performance under the given circumstances of the play. Stanislavsky's "Magic If" is one of the most powerful creative tools to fully engage and stimulate an actor's imagination. Artists and scientists have posed and speculated about the nature of man and the nature of the universe, commencing with the most profound of statements, "What if..."

The inherent creativity of the question "what if" stimulated my imagination in terms of a new way of creating theatre. In the spring of 1991, I was sitting in my living room in Pennsylvania watching television. On this particular Friday night, I was channel surfing with the remote control, seeking some television program that would entertain and engage me. I paused at a channel that appeared to be a local cable station. Immediately, I witnessed a home-shopping type show where the camera shot exhibited a brand-new light blue toilet brush holder for sale. As the TV spokesman's voice droned on and on about the durability of this toilet brush holder, and the camera angle lingered over the static shot, I fell into a state of amazement. Is this what TV had been reduced to? A single continuous shot of a light blue toilet brush holder with an announcer's voice enthusiastically extolling its grand qualities? I rose from my chair and decided to give my dog Brandy his evening walk. As the cool evening air greeted us outside, I started to think about what I had just seen on TV. A single shot of a toilet brush holder! Then, a creative vision seized me - *what if* a group of actors performed scenes on TV under the direction of a drama teacher? The vision became quite clear in my imagination as I finished taking Brandy for his evening walk. That's it, I thought. What if you could direct and produce scenes from theatre on TV in an artistic and educational manner? At this time in my career, I had acted in numerous classical and contemporary plays, dozens of TV commercials, and numerous corporate videos. I had performed in regional, community, and educational theatres, and had acted and modeled in New York, Philadelphia, Atlantic City, and Florida, and was looking for new ways to produce my own artistic projects.

As I entered my home with Brandy my creative vision became even clearer. I would create a TV show about theatre and the dramatic arts, where I would act as the host and drama teacher. My vision became even more specific - I would have student actors perform in short dramatic scenes, no longer than five minutes in length, by such playwrights as Moliere, Shakespeare, Eugene O'Neill, and Tennessee Williams. After each acting scene, I would analyze the performances of the actors, and discuss acting techniques and styles.

The next morning, I called the local cable TV company, and proposed my TV show on the theatre arts. The director of the station greeted my idea with intrigue, then encouragement, and finally acceptance. Thus my TV show on theatre and dramatic arts, *The Culture Corner*, was born. Little did I know how much this cultural TV show would change my artistic life, enhance my acting career, and take me into new, unique, and exciting directions professionally. My first five telecasts would include shows on Improvisation and Acting; Women in Drama: Scenes from American Drama; How to Act in TV Commercials; Classical Comedy: Scenes from Moliere and Shakespeare; and Monologues for the Actor.

The Culture Corner gave me great artistic and creative satisfaction. And to think I had created a respected show on the arts, because I had asked the question "What if" as I walked Brandy on that refreshing spring evening. Indeed, Stanislavsky had a brilliant idea with his concept of "The Magic If."

A creative vision of your theatre is essential in focusing your talents and purposes. At the beginning of this chapter I quoted Goethe, one of the truly great men of the theatre. Johann Wolfgang Von Goethe is a perfect example of a man with a vision for his theatre. Poet and playwright, statesman and scientist, Goethe was a renaissance man of his times. Although the general public is familiar with Goethe as a poet (The Storm and Stress movement of German poetry) and as a playwright(*Faust*), few are aware of his contributions to theatre as a director and theatrical innovator in practical and pragmatic terms.

Goethe transformed the Weimar Court Theatre into one of the most innovative and important theatres of its day. Goethe's vision led him to the development of a finely tuned ensemble acting style, as well as extensive work with actors to rid them of regionalism in their speech. Goethe served as a dramatic coach, helping his actors in terms of developing articulate speech, proper vocal enunciation, and movement styles. Goethe's creative vision led him to introduce practical blocking patterns for his actors, by dividing the stage into squares, thus creating vivid, balanced, and practical theatrical pictorial images for his plays. Goethe's sense of beauty and harmony led him to consult artists concerning the proper theatrical composition of the stage. Along with his artistic associate, the German poet Schiller, Goethe created a theatre that became so famous in Germany and Europe that the term "Weimar Classicism" became synonymous with artistic excellence. Goethe may indeed be one of the world's first modern directors, because of his ability to blend the artistic and technical aspects of theatre into a unifying and aesthetically pleasing whole. Goethe exemplifies to us the importance of a sense of vision for creating theatre. An artist must take those theatrical elements from the past and merge them with his present creative insights in order to forge a theatre for today and tomorrow.

Goethe's observation that "Genius has magic, power, and boldness in it" should reverberate in the depths of our creative minds if we are to imagine and create a theatre for the future.

When Goethe admonishes, inspires, and calls us to fulfill our creative destiny - to "begin it now" - we need to discover and explore the creative vision of our new theatre. For it is this new theatre - a theatre of rich aesthetic possibilities and authentic artistic promise - that will unleash our imaginations and fulfill our creative aspirations. Indeed, we truly need a bold, new vision of drama.

CHAPTER TWO
ACTING WORK:
PLAYS, TV COMMERCIALS, CORPORATE VIDEOS, AND PRINT MODELING

Acting is one of the most difficult ways to earn a living. Perhaps it is *the* most difficult way to generate a consistent, dependable, middle-class income year after year. However, it is possible to find work as an actor in theatre, TV commercials, and corporate videos in today's society if you approach the opportunities in novel and unique ways. Parents heave a collective sigh of disappointment when they learn of their children's aspirations to become actors.

Images of unemployment, underemployment, and abject poverty well up in a parent's mind when they hear the proud proclamation, "I want to be an actor!" from a son or daughter. "Why can't you be an accountant like your cousin Artie?" the parents ask. "He makes good money, and it's a steady job." And, of course, the parents have a point. Statistics each year bear the sad testimony that an actor's life is one of poverty and not riches. The three actor's Unions - The Actor's Equity Association, the Screen Actor's Guild, and the American Federation of Television and Radio Artists, consistently exhibit the grim statistics that at any given time less than 10% of their members are working and making a decent middle class income. So, what's an aspiring actor to do?

First and foremost, not all acting work is union work. True, union acting work pays handsomely and has numerous benefits over nonunion work, but union work can also be elusive, extremely competitive, and very difficult to acquire. However, an actor *can* find an acting job and creative and artistic satisfaction outside of the major markets of New York and Hollywood through nonunion work in plays, TV commercials, corporate videos, and print modeling. This chapter will explore a rich variety of avenues for acting work. There *is* work outside of the major markets in the realm of the artistic activities previously mentioned. However, our discussion of this work will commence with the necessary tools and techniques that an actor needs to get started.

THE HEADSHOT

An actor needs a calling card - a business card - the headshot. Since acting is a visual business, it is imperative that an actor possesses an excellent headshot. In the major markets like New York or Hollywood, headshots can cost anywhere from $275 to $500 and up. However, the focus of this book is on creating work for yourself outside of the major markets, and exploring the talents and services of professionals in the medium-sized markets. I've had headshots made in New York, Philadelphia, Atlantic City, and Florida. I have also received numerous acting jobs from successful headshot-resume submissions. However, I would like to focus on the Philadelphia market for a moment and discuss how an actor can receive an excellent headshot without paying a fortune as he or she would in a major market.

Several years ago, I met a photographer named Art Murphy who specializes in actors' headshots. Art has been a professional photographer for over thirty-four years, and has worked in New York City and Philadelphia. In recent years, Art has focused on the Philadelphia market where he now resides and works. The headshot he took of me in 1998 has helped me book three TV commercials and a major print-modeling job for the State of Pennsylvania. The print ad appears as a billboard throughout the entire state. And, I was paid the princely rate of $1,000 for one hour's worth of work. I am indebted to Art for the excellent headshot, which helped me book the ad. The rates for a headshot in the Philadelphia market are below that of the major markets, and yet a photographer like Art Murphy offers the same high standards of professional excellence.

When asked what makes a great headshot for an actor, Art responded with some acute observations. "A good photo reveals something about the spirit of the person," Art believes. "Acting today is as nonverbal as it is verbal - an actor must have the ability to communicate without saying a word. You have to give people a reason to want to look at you. There must be some feeling of contact and connection. The headshot is for the benefit of revealing the actor's qualities." Art also advises that the headshot should reveal the inner qualities of the actor, "Is this a personable person? Is this a person with an edge? Does this person know how to laugh?" Art asks. "Some people have a quality they can project easily."

The process of getting a good headshot is relatively simple and straightforward. Once an actor goes to the photo session at Art's studio in Philadelphia, Art will take several rolls of film of the actor. The photo session generally lasts one to two hours, and the actor should have a change of wardrobe, excluding all black and white clothing (since the headshot will appear in black and white). Several days later, Art mails the contact sheets to the actor. The actor peruses the contact sheets with a magnifying glass that Art provides, in the attempt to find a good, clean, usable, professional headshot. Many times actors will choose a commercial headshot and a dramatic theatrical shot. "Decisions of the final headshot should be made by agents, acting teachers, actors, and people in the field," Art advises. "Sweethearts and family members may not understand the needs of the business."

Once the actor orders the final 8 x 10 black-and-white print from the contact sheet, she then sends it to a reproduction house (I recommend many of the fine photo-reproduction houses in New York City; they generally do an excellent job and understand the marketplace).

The headshot can have a glossy or matte finish, with or without a border, and of course, it should appear in black and white. The final aesthetic decisions ultimately come from the actor, since this is your professional calling card. One of the most frequently asked questions I receive from drama students is what to do with the headshots when they are received from the reproduction house. The 100 8 x 10 black-and-white headshots will come back from the reproduction house within a week or so. As stated previously, headshots are the calling cards of the acting business, and they need to look as professional as possible. Since many acting jobs can be booked directly from the headshot and resume, it is imperative that you send the photos to people who will hire and give you the acting work you desire.

WHERE TO SEND YOUR HEADSHOTS

If you live in a city like Philadelphia, Boston, Baltimore, Atlantic City, Washington, D.C., Atlanta, or Tampa (as well as similar cities), you might want to consider sending your headshot and resumes to the following people and places:

- 10 copies to talent agents in your area
- 10 copies to film and video companies
- 10 copies to advertising agencies
- 10 copies to TV stations, including local and cable stations
- 10 copies to theatres (local and regional)
- 10 copies to photographers who work in commercial print modeling
- 10 copies to casting directors
- 10 copies to major corporations that have a corporate video division

And, it's important to keep twenty copies for yourself since you will need them for auditions. You will need to reorder another 100 headshots as the demand for your work and services as an actor grows.

The previous list of where to send your headshots is based on years and years of professional experience. The rationale for my list of people and places to send your headshots can be succinctly summarized as thus:

You will need to send copies to agents in your area who will represent you and submit you for acting work. You only need one agent, but many times you can multiple list with agents, thereby increasing your chances for different jobs and a greater variety of work. Some agents discourage multiple listing, but while you are starting your career, you don't have much to lose by listing with more than one agent.

You will also need to send your headshot and resume to film and video production companies in your area - many times they will go through their files when casting a project and book you directly. I have been booked for a TV commercial and two corporate videos directly from local film and video production houses that had my headshot and resume in their files.

It is also a good idea to send your headshot and resumes to local advertising agencies, since many times they represent the client who is making the TV commercial, corporate video, or print ad. Remember to send your photos to the major ad agencies in your area. It's always an intelligent idea to call and see if they are involved in corporate and commercial work. Also, local TV stations can hire you directly as an actor, so it's worth getting the name of the station director, and sending him your headshot and resume.

Since local theatres hire actors and sometimes pay actors, it is essential that you send your photo-resume to the producers of the theatre. You may also mail your headshot to photographers who specialize in or shoot print-modeling jobs. Since commercial print modeling can pay anywhere from $125 to $1,000 an hour (with buyouts), actors need to explore this avenue of work as well.

Casting Directors are certainly important to an actor's career; therefore, it's imperative that you get your headshot and resume into the hands of the people who actually cast plays, TV commercials, corporate videos, and print ads. Also, major corporations will have separate divisions for corporate video production, and this should be an avenue that is explored.

And finally, it's important to keep at least twenty

headshots for yourself in the event of auditions and other direct submissions. These recommendations constitute my professional opinion, and submissions of headshots and resumes to these people and places have spelled acting work for me with many lucrative and wonderful jobs.

Now, let's take a specific look at some of the types of acting work you can find outside of the major markets.

ACTING IN PLAYS

The Hedgerow Theatre is a resident repertory theatre located in Rose Valley, Pennsylvania. Founded by Jasper Deeter in 1923, this unique artistically respected theatre has been an authentic cultural landmark for the past seventy-five years in Southeastern Pennsylvania.

"Our artistic goals are to be a part of the community. We are a nonprofit organization dedicated to a wide variety of theatrical experiences," explains Matthew Daciuk, an actor and sound designer at the Hedgerow Theatre. Matthew has nearly a decade of theatrical experience and has been trained at the Hedgerow Theatre's training program. Matthew has appeared in *As You Like It*, *Hamlet*, *Androcles and the Lion*, and numerous children's productions at Hedgerow.

Matthew describes the Hedgerow Theatre as, "A great place for actors to build experience. We look for actors who have room to grow. Hedgerow is an educational theatrical training ground of sorts. We have a theatre school that is quite popular." Since the Hedgerow Theatre is artistically and culturally dedicated to quality, the theatre offers a wide range of plays to audiences: the classics, mysteries, contemporary works, children's plays, and some controversial shows as well.

"We hold yearly auditions for actors. Generally, we advertise in *Backstage* or other theatre-related publications," Matthew explains. "We look for actors with potential and the ability to grow. Although many of the actors are previously trained, Hedgerow develops their acting even more. Hedgerow helps to develop an appreciation for theatre as an institution."

The actors are residents who live and work together. They become true practitioners of theatre, since they have responsibilities outside the realm of acting. Many of the actors learn the technical aspects of theatre as well: lighting, sound, publicity, set construction, and the intricacies of theatre as an institution and an art form. As a nonunion theatre, the Hedgerow pays a small salary to actors when they perform in plays. Like most nonunion theatres, actors receive a salary for their creative efforts. However, the rates vary widely from theatre to theatre, depending on the theatre's size, budget, and audience.

The Gateway Playhouse, located in Somers Point, New Jersey, is yet another fine example of a small theatre with high artistic aspirations and a commitment to creatively exciting theatrical productions. General Manager and Producer, Bill Marshall, observes that the artistic goal of his theatre is, "to make sure that the shows are fun to watch! Period! We want the audience to leave the theatre smiling or whistling a happy tune. We produce musicals and comedies. We look for actors with energy - physical and mental energy - and the ability to project, while even standing still."

Located in Southern New Jersey, within minutes of such resorts as Ocean City and Atlantic City, The Gateway Theatre offers audiences the opportunity to attend theatre while vacationing at the beautiful Jersey shore. As a small theatre with high standards, Bill makes some acute observations about the state of acting and the nature of nonunion theatres. "When we audition, we take the best the theatre can afford. In an audition, I look for attitude and confidence - even in an untrained actor. Talent does not always own a card. I have never heard of anyone getting a card first, and then acting. Talent is talent - trained or not."

Generally, there are two ways to get involved in a nonunion theatre. Look for open auditions that are advertised in newspapers and theatre-related publications. At an open audition, an actor will have to perform two monologues: one dramatic, and one comedic. One monologue should be from a classical work such as Shakespeare, Euripides, Sophocles, Racine or one the classical masters, while the other monologue should be from a contemporary work. It is important that the monologues be *contrasting* in tone and intent, thus exhibiting an actor's emotional and artistic range. Many times, theatres will hold auditions for specific plays, and an actor will attend the audition with the goal of reading from the specific play that is being produced. At any rate, it is essential that an actor is familiar with a large body of dramatic work. It is imperative that actors read plays - the classical works as well as modern works. And it is essential that actors *see* as many plays as they can possibly attend.

In order to get in plays, an actor should be truly cultured and well educated in all the arts. Actors will be called upon to perform roles from the very history of theatre, and so an actor needs to become self-educated and sensitive to all the arts. Actors should attend as many cultural events as they can - art museums, art galleries, the opera, concerts, and any other rich cultural experience that will broaden an actor's understanding of the world. Acting in plays requires that actors have an understanding of art, literature, history, philosophy, religion, and the sciences.

Actors need to tune their imaginations and instruments if they are to succeed in the realm of theatre. The creative imagination of the actor is fed by those rich cultural and artistic experiences previously mentioned. The actor's instrument (the body and voice) needs to be finely tuned so that she can make exciting, creative choices in the roles she performs. Acting in plays is creatively demanding, and an actor needs to be well trained and well versed in the theatre. Acting in plays is artistically rewarding, because it allows the actor to use his entire being in the creation of a role. Stage acting allows an actor to explore the depths of his psychological, spiritual, and intellectual being. Acting on stage enables an actor to use her entire being in a creative and imaginatively fulfilling manner.

Acting in plays enables actors to pursue their

objectives and goals in a through-line of moments every evening of the show. The energy between actor and audience is the true magic of theatre, and is what makes acting in plays so very special.

ACTING IN TV COMMERCIALS

"Actors must be able to project a complete three-dimensional character in thirty seconds or less," observes Debra Glass, an experienced producer and director of TV commercials. "An actor must be creative with whatever material is given to him or her. Sometimes the script may not make sense to them, or may seem silly. But the opinion of an actor is not needed or desired at an audition. What directors want to see, is an actor who can fulfill the requirements of the script in a unique and exciting way. Actors must also remember that there may be many takes, and they must be able to do a scene with the same amount of freshness and spontaneity on the fiftieth take as they did on the first," she advises.

A producer and director of independent video projects with more than ten years of TV production experience, Debra Glass has directed over sixty-five local and regional TV commercials. Debra is also an actress who has appeared in numerous community plays and local television shows for the last twenty years. A graduate of Kutztown University, with a Bachelor of Science degree in Telecommunications, Debra holds many unique perspectives on acting and television commercial work. "Auditions can be a daunting and difficult experience for everyone. However, it is the director and producer's job to find those people that can make a script come alive. Sometimes the characters in a script are widely drawn and can be played by many different types, and sometimes the script is extremely specific about the characters needed. When I cast a TV commercial I'm looking for what's appropriate by type, age, and performance ability, and if I find someone that meets those requirements and they offer a unique spark, I'm thrilled," Debra explains.

Debra stresses the need for actors to create characters and project their characters clearly and creatively in the thirty seconds that TV commercials provide. It is essential for actors to think of TV commercials as mini-plays. Like a play, the actor has to have an objective, a motivation, and a purpose · for his playing. An actor has to tap into the same fundamental principles for creating a character in a play: Who am I? What do I want? In addition to these basic acting questions, the actor has to project her personality effectively and effortlessly. Since television is a medium of personality, an actor has to learn to use the core of his natural charisma and personality as well in the realm of commercials.

Acting in television commercials allows an actor to create a character using vivid and specific choices. TV commercials generally have a beginning, middle, and an end, much like a play. Goals and motivations must be played with the same creative insight as developing a character in a play. However, in this case, the "play" is a mini-play of thirty seconds. It's absolutely essential then for actors to create specific characters immediately, and to exhibit their motivations as soon as possible. It *is* possible for an actor to project a character in the thirty seconds of the commercial, but it requires authentic acting skills and abilities. Every glance and gesture that an actor makes in a TV commercial has an impact, and so it is important for the actor to have clear intentions and objectives. Every glance and gesture should build the character effectively so that the audience understands the character in the commercial immediately. "An actor needs to express as full a character as possible even if they appear on the screen for ten seconds," Debra observes.

Actors have to be fully engaged in the moment, and TV commercials are really snapshots of "moments" in life. The ultimate purpose of TV commercials is, of course, to sell something to the consumer in a creative and engaging way. And so, to succeed in this acting specialty, you must immediately create a believable character, and project this character in an amusing, witty, charming, and imaginative manner.

Acting in TV commercials, can help actors to hone their acting and vocal skills. Articulation and vocal fluency are essential for an actor performing in a commercial, since many times an actor will serve as a spokesperson for a product. Credibility is the key, if the audience is to truly believe the actor embraces and endorses the particular product.

Theatre work - acting in plays - is great training for acting in TV commercials. However, there are classes for TV commercial acting offered in many cities. The Weist-Barron School of Television Acting in New York is one of the finest commercial schools of its kind. Weist-Barron offers TV commercials and workshops for all aspects of this form of acting work. And, Weist-Barron has several satellite schools scattered throughout the country. An actor aspiring to succeed in TV commercials should study theatre and complement his training with commercial classes from a reputable school or workshop.

Nonunion TV commercials pay a flat rate to the actor as opposed to the lucrative residuals received from a union TV commercial. The rates can range from $250 and up for a local or regional TV commercial. Acting in TV commercials can give an actor excellent exposure, since even in a mid-size city, the metropolitan area can encompass a million or more people. And, casting directors can see an actor's work in a successful regional TV commercial. Therefore, acting in TV commercials offers exposure, experience, and economic opportunity for an actor.

Further benefits from acting in TV commercials include the creative opportunity to hone improvisational skills. Many times, actors don't have dialogue in commercials, and they have to perform or mime actions. Versatility and adaptability are important assets for actors working in commercials, and they must take direction well.

Generally, a TV commercial can be shot in a few hours to a single day. Actors generally receive their scripts a few days in advance. It is imperative that an actor has the lines of the script fully memorized before the actual shoot. At the rehearsal, the director will go over the interpretation of the commercial copy, and direct the actor to the appropriate physical and vocal actions - the "business" of the TV commercial. Since film and TV is a director's medium, it's essential that the actor take careful direction from the producer or director in charge. However, it's important for an actor to bring some creative choices to the TV commercial.

Getting cast in a TV commercial can occur in several ways. The agent representing an actor can submit the headshot and resume to a casting director, client, or ad agency that then hires the actor on the strength of her "type" and photo-resume. An actor can also be called in by a casting director to audition for the commercial, along with dozens of other actors who fall into the appropriate "type" or category for the commercial. Actors can also submit their headshots and resumes to local directors of cable TV stations or directors of video production companies. Acting in TV commercials should be an adjunct to acting in plays, and provides valuable experience and exposure for actors.

CORPORATE VIDEOS

"A corporate video is a non-broadcast program that could have one of several uses," observes Jim Grey, the producer and director of VideoWorks Production Company in Reading, Pennsylvania. "A corporate video can be used as a sales tool, or it can be used for promotional purposes. Corporate videos can have small budgets or huge budgets. There are different levels of work available for actors, and it's a great way to get acting experience," Jim advises.

A graduate of Kutztown University, with a Bachelor of Science degree in Telecommunications, Jim has been a director and producer of corporate, industrial, and commercial videos for over thirteen years. As a director of videography for several companies ranging from cable advertising to local broadcast, Jim has had a wealth of experience in this field. Several years ago, Jim created his own company, VideoWorks, bringing his rich experience and education to the growing field of videography.

When asked what some of the intrinsic difficulties for actors performing in corporate videos were, Jim provided some acute insights. "Some of the challenges for actors in corporate videos are having them fit into a situation they've never been in before, or operating equipment they're not familiar with - but they have to look natural when performing these activities, and not look like they're acting."

Occasionally, companies will try to use employees in their corporate videos, yet it rarely meets with the same kind of success. "It's a real benefit to have an actor in a corporate video," Jim observes. "You need an actor who can take direction well. An actor will do a take perhaps five times, as opposed to the fifty takes it may take from an employee."

However, there are challenges for an actor performing in corporate videos as well. Jim notes that these challenges can include "...an unfamiliar environment. You're not always on a set. A corporate video can take place on the work site, on location, or at the factory." Yet Jim observes that there are numerous rewards in the realm of acting in corporate videos. "You learn about other aspects of life - it can be interesting work, and it's a good place for an actor to get started, and build experience.

Acting in corporate videos can truly build an actor's resume. "If an actor hasn't had a lot of experience, it can be a real break," Jim observes. "It's an opportunity to act in front of the camera and learn many useful techniques." Indeed, corporate videos can offer almost the same experience as acting in a movie. Like a movie, a corporate video can include a crew that consists of a director, a sound- and light technician, a make-up artist, an assistant director, and a script supervisor. Actors generally receive their scripts a few days in advance, and are expected to have their lines memorized so they are ready to perform the day of the shoot. Rehearsals generally occur in front of the camera at the location.

The financial rewards for corporate videos are also evident. Actors can receive anywhere from $200 to $800 a day for a nonunion corporate video. Many corporate videos are multiple day shoots, so an actor can make good money in this field. My first corporate video acting experience occurred in 1984, and was filmed in Sarasota, Florida. I was paid $200 a day for the four-day shoot and learned many valuable camera-acting techniques. Medical corporate videos can pay as much as $700 to $800 a day, because of the difficult technical terms intrinsic to the language of medicine.

There are numerous kinds of corporate videos as well. I've acted in over thirty-five corporate videos including videos for hospitals, educational institutions, banks, pharmaceutical companies, foundations, drug rehabilitation clinics, car companies, condominium associations, and medical training videos. As you can see, corporate videos offer a wealth of opportunities for the actor, but flexibility, versatility, and adaptability are the keys to a successful career in corporate video acting. Since the dialogue in corporate videos can be very difficult for an actor to deliver - he must learn the techniques of living truthfully under the given circumstances, moment by moment. There are times when an actor will not - in fact, cannot - fully comprehend the meaning of the highly technical terms or highly specialized vocabulary inherent to corporate videos. It is wise for the actor to invest in the relationship with the other actor - the rich emotional interplay that will make the communication credible, believable, and natural in the corporate video. Here is a sample script of a corporate video, providing the inherent problems of these specialized scripts:

Bill: I'm glad you've taken the time to go over the annual incentive compensation pay program with me. I'm *still* having problems with some key elements.

Debra: No problem, Bill. It will be my pleasure to help you and your department go over the incentive compensation plan program and the PASCAL project.

Bill: You know, Debra, I'm not very good with the numbers. In fact, I always forget whether the incentive plan is paid for one-fourth or one-fifth of the total amount of the program.

Debra: Yes, that happens to me sometimes. Just remember that the bonus for the PASCAL project is one-fourth of the annual earnings for the incentive compensation plan program. And, you'll need to keep in mind, any payments from the WHT plan program as well.

PASCAL project? The WHT plan program? And

what exactly is the incentive compensation plan program? As an actor in corporate videos, you will encounter and have to embrace these challenges. Once again, the key is creating a credible character and investing in the relationship with the other actor. Living truthfully under the given circumstances will go a long, long way in transcending the highly specialized dialogue. Make sure you do as much research and ask as many questions as you can to the client or the director of the project.

As stated earlier, corporate videos are largely shot on location at the corporation, Auto Company, or hospital. Corporate videos can be shot outside in any kind of weather, and this is an obvious challenge that actors must cope with and embrace. Once again, corporate videos can mimic movies and feature films in this respect. Also, like movies, corporate video scripts are shot out of sequence at different locations. For this reason, it is imperative that actors realize and understand the objectives and motivations of their characters.

Another important aspect of acting in corporate videos is that they can be videotaped virtually anywhere. I've acted in corporate videos in such states as Florida, Delaware, New Jersey, and Pennsylvania. Since the goal of this book is to help actors find acting work outside of the major markets, corporate videos provide truly excellent experience.

When an actor performs in enough corporate videos, he can have a demo video made of the various scenes of their most polished performances in corporate videos. Indeed, corporate videos offer actors artistic and economic opportunities to enhance their resumes and their experience.

COMMERCIAL PRINT MODELING

In early 1988 one of my Philadelphia agents submitted my photo-resume to a New York modeling agent without my knowledge. Unexpectedly, I received a phone call one day from the New York agent wanting to meet with me concerning something called "Commercial Print." A week later, I made the trip to New York City to meet with my first commercial print modeling agent, Carl Landreth of Looks Agency.

Although I had acted in countless plays, and numerous TV commercials by then, and had done some modeling, I was unfamiliar with this particular form of commercial work. Since most people are familiar with fashion modeling, and the moody, beautiful gazes of fashion models from magazine covers or billboards, the general public is less familiar with print modeling or commercial print modeling as it is often called.

The purpose of commercial print modeling is to sell a product, a service, or goods in the market place. Generally, fashion modeling has as its goal to sell fashion, beauty products, or an attitude. Commercial print modeling aspires to sell some product or service to the consumer. Actors can do extremely well in commercial print modeling because photographic "scenes" are created, and the actor must improvise under the given circumstance in the specific situation. Acting skills are important for a print model, since the "scene" has to seem real and authentic.

Joel Zarska is a prominent photographer who was trained in New York City and now resides and works in Berks County, Pennsylvania. With over twenty-one years in the business, Joel has worked in fashion, print, and catalogues. He sees the wisdom of using actors for commercial print work because they know "how to give a variety of expressions." A successful actor in print modeling must learn "to generate the mood in order to sell the product." Joel also believes that, "It's important for an actor to be comfortable in front of a camera. The actor or model can't upstage the product, nor can they have too strong of a personality."

However, Joel observes that it's important for the actor/print model "to look intelligent, and possess a photogenic quality. Good bone structure is also important," he adds. The all-American look is a popular look in print. Clean cut. Wholesome. Attractive. And of course a successful actor in print should portray a positive attitude. An actor who can fit into a specific "type" has a good chance of getting work. Types can include the pretty housewife, the good looking all-American dad, the clean-cut successful yuppie, the happy helpful grandmother, and the cute, wholesome girl or boy to name but a few. Acting is a business of "types" and it's important that an actor plays to his strengths in this realm.

The financial rewards for commercial print modeling can be extremely lucrative. Since models are paid by the hour for a job, a commercial print model can earn anywhere from $125 an hour to $1,000 an hour *outside* of a major market like New York City, (where the rates are $250 an hour and up). An actor who works in print modeling can receive bonus buyouts for her job, depending on the specific contract for the job. I have had print modeling jobs that have paid $300 to even $1,000 an hour. Agents generally receive 20% of the actor's gross income, and it can take two to three months to be paid for the specific job.

The variety of print ads is enormous. Personally, I have appeared in over 200 commercial print modeling jobs. I have appeared in print ads for windows, mattresses, motels, restaurants, banks, business machines, farm equipment, candy, insurance fraud, hospitals, health care systems, and computers. I've appeared in national prints ads, billboards, brochures, newspapers, magazines, trade and tourist books, and annual reports for companies. Print ads can give actors an enormous amount of exposure, as well as building your bank account and portfolio.

To succeed in commercial print modeling, you'll need an excellent headshot, a composite card, an agent, a varied wardrobe (actors and models have to supply their own clothes many times), a portfolio, and a good, positive attitude. Print modeling gives an actor the opportunity to improvise under the given circumstances and to take direction on cue from the photographer or art director.

Commercial print modeling is an excellent avenue for an actor to gain experience improvising under the direction of a photographer and director. And, as stated before, it can be very lucrative. Print modeling also allows the actor to create characters, and since this is the ultimate goal and artistic responsibility of the actor, commercial print helps to fit the bill.

Since actors are unemployed between acting jobs, commercial print modeling can certainly fill the gaps, helping to hone one's acting ability, and always boosting their bank accounts.

These then, are some of the creative avenues and exciting opportunities for actors: acting in plays, performing in TV commercials, corporate videos, and print modeling.

Since acting is one of the most challenging businesses in the world, I've come up with a series of questions to stimulate an actor's imagination concerning her motivations for being in this business. Here then are my "reality check" questions for the aspiring performer.

- Do you feel lucky?

- Do you gamble with all your Monopoly money when it's on Park Place?

- Do you like tuna? Night after night?

- Do you like Skippy? (Not the man - the peanut butter)

- Do you enjoy living with your parents at the age of 37?

- Is middle-class comfort important to you? A nice house, a car, and cash in the bank?

- Do you like credit - good credit, that is?

  Seriously though, these questions are intended to stimulate an actor into action - into making contacts and finding work that can result in your ultimate artistic and commercial success.

CHAPTER THREE
EDUCATION AND TRAINING

Education. You need it. Training. It's absolutely essential. An actor needs to be trained and educated. Pure and simple. First and foremost, high schools across the country generally provide some form of dramatic training through either formal drama classes or play productions.

Aspiring actors should start in theatre, and acting in a high school play is an excellent idea for a budding thespian. Generally, high schools offer introductory drama and speech classes that give beginning actors a chance to explore their imaginations and instruments. High schools usually produce a play each semester, and rehearsals for students occur after school and in the evening. Acting in high school plays offers students valuable opportunities for artistic growth and creative development. Many times high schools participate in play competitions, and this offers further artistic development and aesthetic experience.

FORMAL EDUCATION

College programs offer a wide variety of options for young actors. Generally, there are two educational avenues for an aspiring actor to take: the

Bachelor of Arts degree or the Bachelor of Fine Arts degree. There are specific distinctions between these educational programs, so let's take a closer look at the goals and objectives of these programs.

THE BACHELOR OF ARTS

The Bachelor of Arts degree in theatre offers students a broad-based liberal arts education. Courses in literature, history, psychology, sociology, philosophy, religion, and art complement courses in acting, theatre history, dramatic literature, play production, directing, and design. There's much to be said for a good, solid liberal arts education. Students are exposed to the classics, the arts, and the sciences in the overall structure of the humanities. Since actors have to portray a variety of roles in their careers, and create a rich array of characters, a liberal arts education provides aspiring actors with an understanding of human nature and the human condition. A Bachelor of Arts degree is an academic degree with a stress on scholastics and not performance. A graduate with a Bachelor of Arts should pursue either graduate work (the MA or the MFA) or some kind of conservatory training.

San Jose State University offers the Bachelor of Arts degree in drama and radio-television broadcasting. "Our 'hands - on' program allows students to pursue a number of academic paths, to delve deeply into a particular interest, or to diversify and test the waters of several related disciplines," comments Dr. Robert Jenkins, chairman of the theatre arts department at San Jose State University in San Jose, California. The courses leading to the BA in Theatre Arts and Drama include acting, theatre appreciation, script analysis, voice and diction, make-up for stage, film, and television, as well as courses in directing and musical theatre.

Dr. Jenkins observes that, "We have become increasingly focused on video and film production for television and multimedia, and our actors and crews spend more time in front of and behind the camera every year." A member of the San Jose State University Theatre Arts faculty for over twenty-five years, Dr. Jenkins teaches courses in acting, directing, theatre appreciation, and storytelling. He served as the associate dean of humanities and the arts, as well as the director of theatre production at the university.

"As a producing theatre, we present an annual season of live stage plays and numerous studio and student directed projects," Dr. Jenkins explains.

San Jose State University is located in the Silicon Valley and provides students with a rich environment of cultural and technological innovation.

THE BACHELOR OF FINE ARTS

The Bachelor of Fine Arts, or BFA as it is often called, is a theatre degree that is performance oriented. A BFA degree stresses a variety of courses in performance - acting, voice, speech, movement, dance, mime, fencing, and other courses that promote special theatrical skills. There is far less focus on traditional academic subjects in the BFA course of study. However, there will be a core requirement of courses. Once again, it's important to remember that the Bachelor of Fine Arts is performance and not academically oriented. There are pros and cons to each of the degrees - the BA in theatre or the BFA. It depends on what the aspiring actor wishes to focus on during her college career, and which, if any, advanced degrees the student intends to seek.

THE MASTER OF ARTS

The Master of Arts degree in Theatre is an academic degree that focuses on the cultural, artistic, literary, and educational aspects of theatre. A core requirement of courses includes dramatic literature, theatre history, acting, and script analysis.

Complimentary courses include performance theory, dramaturgy, scene design, directing, and playwriting.

Villanova University offers a Master of Arts degree in Theatre and has earned an excellent reputation for its graduate program. Father Peter Donohue is the chairman of the theatre department; he offers several important insights about Villanova's Theatre program and the purpose of educational theatre.

"In an educational institution, we want our students to be exposed to theatre throughout the ages," Father Donohue explains. "Educational theatre gives us a lot more freedom than a commercial theatre has - the university supports our artistic efforts. We want to offer our students and our audiences a variety of theatrical experiences."

Villanova University balances its theatre season with a unique variety of classical and contemporary plays. "We can do a number of different kinds of plays that would not be produced by a commercial theatre," Father Donohue observes. "Villanova encourages new playwrights. We have produced plays by such prominent playwrights as David Rabe, Leslie Lee, and Bruce Graham. We offer the possibilities of experimental work, new work, and classical work."

The Master of Arts degree is excellent preparation for an actor working in theatre or teaching theatre at the high school, community college, or university level. The Master of Arts is not a terminal degree, and, sometimes, graduate students will pursue a PhD upon completion of the Master of Arts degree. It has been my experience that a terminal degree is necessary for a full-time teaching position at the University level. Villanova University's Master of Arts degree is a program that combines scholarly studies with the practical application of theatre. The graduate students study world theatre and drama in a critical and creative manner. Plays from the Western tradition are studied as well as plays from the East. The Master of Arts degree at Villanova provides the necessary artistic and aesthetic experiences for a theatre educator, scholar, or practitioner.

Villanova University is located fifteen miles from the city of Philadelphia, along the Main Line, and it is one of the region's finest universities. The metropolitan area hosts a variety of cultural and artistic activities that complement any student's educational experience. There are theatres, art museums, art galleries, and musical events close to this excellent educational institution. The Mainline is a beautiful area and there are numerous colleges and universities within a ten-mile radius.

To qualify for MA studies, most theatre departments require a Bachelor's degree from an accredited college or university with a satisfactory academic record. The MA in Theatre requirement is a minimum of thirty-three credit hours plus participation in the various theatrical productions. Comprehensive examinations in dramatic literature and theatre history are given in lieu of the traditional thesis. Students are encouraged to participate in either the artistic or technical end of the productions each semester.

THE MASTER OF FINE ARTS

The Florida State University offers the Master of Fine Arts degree in Acting. This MFA theatre program is associated with the highly acclaimed Asolo Theatre Company - Florida's regional repertory theatre - located in beautiful Sarasota, Florida. The MFA in Acting program is a three-year training program that aspires to train candidates for careers in acting and theatre.

"The FSU/Asolo Conservatory is the kind of place where a student actor becomes part of a very close knit family. The faculty is a very positive, unpretentious and cohesive group that shares a common definition of good acting, which is the foundation of every class we teach," observes Brant

L. Pope, director of the Florida State University/Asolo Conservatory program.

The first year of the MFA in Acting program includes courses in acting, voice, movement, dramatic literature, and rehearsal and performance. The second year of the program extends the foundation of acting courses and enables students to perform major roles in a four-play season. The end of the second year of acting training takes the MFA students to the FSU London Study Center. This nine-week residency in London, England, allows the students to become exposed to the rich cultural activities of London's theatres, museums, art galleries, and historical landmarks. The acting training focuses on the comedic styles of Restoration plays. These bold comedies flourished on the British stage during the seventeenth and eighteenth centuries and are still very popular today. At the London Center, the acting, voice, and speech classes focus on this dynamic period of dramatic literature.

During the third year of study, the students become associate members of the resident acting company of the Asolo Theatre. This innovative and unique association allows the students to train and work with professional Equity actors. The students are presented the opportunity to act in several productions on the professional stage and become eligible to join Actors Equity Association at the end of the three-year program.

"Upon this base we give our students the skills and techniques to act successfully in any period and style. These skills, then, are put to the test as they take their place and the stage as members of the Asolo Theatre Company," explains Brant Pope.

The acting courses at the FSU/Asolo Conservatory include the basic principles of acting, the study of contemporary and classic Realism, studies in style and performance, and the study of Shakespeare. The voice classes focus on the fundamentals of vocal production, as well as phonetics, diction, verse, dialects, and singing skills. The movement classes focus on body and movement fundamentals, as well as dance and period movement styles. The MFA in Acting program enables students to become immersed in the total theatrical experience.

"The most important goal of our training program is the teaching of a process or 'way of working' that an actor can use throughout his or her career. We pledge to our students that we will not focus on directing you, but rather concentrate on helping you to learn a systematic way of responding to those people who will be directing you," Mr. Pope explains.

The very location of the Asolo Theatre in Sarasota, Florida is yet another example of this distinctive theatrical program. The word Asolo is derived from Asolo, Italy, where this beautiful eighteenth-century theatre was housed until it was purchased and moved by the John Ringling estate more than forty years ago to its present location in Sarasota. The Asolo Theatre is part of a cultural complex that includes the Ringling Art Museum and Gardens. The Art Museum includes one of the largest collections of Baroque Art in the country, as well as many masterpieces by Peter Paul Rubens. Situated on scenic Sarasota Bay, the Asolo Theatre is a vital, creative force in the artistic community of Sarasota, Florida. This charming, small city hosts numerous cultural attractions, including its own opera, a symphony, a ballet, and numerous theatres. This cultured community provides an excellent artistic atmosphere for an aspiring thespian.

The admissions requirements to the FSU/Asolo Conservatory include an audition and interview that may be held privately at the Conservatory or arranged at the University Resident Theatre Association in New York. Students must have a BA or its equivalent from an accredited college or university, a GPA of 3.0 or better, and a combined score of 1,000 on the Graduate Record Examination. Stipends and financial aid are available in this program. The MFA in Acting degree will enable students to employ their skills in the professional realm of theatre or the academic realm as a professional educator.

THE PhD IN THEATRE

The PhD in Theatre prepares students as teachers or scholars of Theatre. An MA degree in theatre or an MFA degree in Drama along with writing samples, letters of recommendation, GRE scores, and experience are required for admission to a PhD program in Theatre. The University of Maryland, located in College Park, Maryland offers a PhD in Theatre. Each doctoral student takes a variety of courses in theatre and research. The University of Maryland offers such courses as introduction to doctoral studies in theatre, critical methods in theatre, historiography and historical methods in theatre, and doctoral dissertation research. Prior to writing a dissertation, each doctoral student is expected to have a reading knowledge of two languages. The PhD in Theatre is a competency-based degree, and the doctoral candidate must complete the dissertation within four years of passing the comprehensive exam. The PhD is an academic and scholarly degree that aspires to train professors of theatre for teaching at the college or university level.

COMMERCIAL CLASSES

Actors need some kind of training whether they attend the formal experience of a college education or not. Theatre workshops and commercial classes are offered in most major cities in the United States. It is a wise idea to take drama classes from time to time in order to learn new techniques, hone acting skills, and stay fresh in the field. Commercial classes can range from beginning classes in acting and scene study to TV commercial and film acting classes.

One of the finest commercial schools in the country for the study of TV commercials and film acting techniques is the Weist-Barron School of Television. Located in mid-town Manhattan, the Weist-Barron school is centrally and vitally situated in New York City - the communications, theatre, and art capital of America. The teachers are working directors and actors in New York and the region, and this gives the school an edge, since the teachers are actively engaged in the field. The teachers are generous in sharing valuable techniques and tips for the acting business. The Weist-Barron School of Television offers courses in TV commercial techniques, soap opera acting techniques, and scene study. There are classes for adults and teens offered at different times of the day and evening. Classes are ongoing throughout the year, and this school benefits greatly from its excellent instructors and dynamic location in one of the world's most exciting cities. The Weist-Barron school has satellite schools throughout the United States, and these schools offer many of the same commercial courses. The TV commercial classes at Weist-Barron are truly the finest classes of their kind, and students are given ample time in front of the camera to learn the essential techniques of commercial acting. If you desire to act in TV commercials, the Weist-Barron School is an excellent school in which to learn the fundamental techniques of this acting subcraft.

Valerie Adami, director of programs, observes that the Weist-Barron School aspires "to give the very best in training, information and emotional support to every actor who comes here. Absolutely anyone of any type can be the perfect choice for a commercial in today's diverse market. Actors are often interested and willing to pursue commercials because of the enormous financial benefits. Therefore - learn what you need to know, and get out there and book!"

Weist-Barron has schools in Atlantic City, New

Jersey and Burbank, California. Founded by Dwight Weist and Bob Barron about forty years ago, this unique school offers students many creative opportunities. Valerie Adami explains, "Dwight Weist and Bob Barron were pioneers in the TV commercial business. Newcomers and even ordinary people were great sources for this new burgeoning industry. Bob and Dwight were innovative, creative men, very good at what they did and both gifted instructors. They devised accessible, informative, and fun courses that made the actor feel comfortable in front of the camera and confident in copy interpretation."

Ms. Adami says that "every actor has a unique quality all their own. What we and everyone else in the industry responds to the most is TALENT! For the most part, commercial actors are chosen to portray exactly who they appear to be in terms of age, look and emotional quality. Classical actors may reinvent themselves to do any number of dramatic (comedic) interpretations depending on the part they have been cast in. Also to sustain a performance for the stage or even for film, the actor requires significant training and experience."

Ms. Adami also observes "traditional commercial actors should possess qualities like ability, warmth, sincerity, honesty, and humor."

The Weist-Barron School of Acting is a great training ground for the aspiring actor.

ADDITIONAL TRAINING

The actor's instrument - the body and voice - must be well trained and tuned. Therefore, it is imperative that an actor seeks training in the realms of voice, speech, and movement. Articulate speech and proper vocal production is absolutely essential if an actor is to convey subtle nuances and creative meanings in the dramatic text effectively and imaginatively. An actor's voice is his own unique signature in the realm of character creation. Actors should complement their classical and commercial training with studies in voice and speech. Let's take a look at some voice and speech exercises that can increase an actor's vocal power and promote articulate speech. The following vocal and articulation exercises should be practiced frequently and with diligence in order to achieve greater control of the instrument. You may wish to practice these sentences ten to fifteen minutes each day for maximum power and effectiveness.

- MA - MAY - MEE - MO - MOO

- The tip of the teeth, the lips, and the tongue.

- Delightful Dodie doubted the National Debt as she dove into the deep blue Ocean.

- Darling Debra dug the deepest ditches in Des Moines.

- Tenacious Terry took time to travel down the Thames.

- Brandy Dandy brought dandy presents to the pleasant picnic.

Classes in singing, speech, and voice can only aid an aspiring actor in achieving her full vocal power and range. Another idea and technique for an actor to explore is reciting poetry aloud everyday. The power and beauty of poetry has inspired humanity from the beginning of time. Poetry, especially poems with a multiplicity of rich vowel sounds, is an effective and pleasant way to improve an actor's voice and speech.

The poetry of Shakespeare and the Romantic poets - Shelley, Byron, Keats, and Coleridge - is particularly effective in producing vocal fluency and articulate speech. The following lines from some of the world's most beautiful poetry should aid in your development as an actor. Practice of these lines of verse everyday should give more power, depth, and beauty to your speech.

- Wild West Wind, thou breath of Autumn's being, Thou, from whose unseen presence the leaves dead are driven ... (Percy Bysshe Shelley)

- Season of mists and mellow fruitfulness, Close bosom-friend of the maturing sun ... (John Keats)

- She walks in beauty, like the night of cloudless climes and starry skies; and all that's best of dark and her eyes ... (Lord Byron)
- Not marble, nor the gilded monuments of princes, shall outlive this powerful rhyme ... (William Shakespeare)

The practice of reading poetry aloud every day should develop an actor's vocal range and fluency immensely. Select poetry that you love and find uplifting, and make a commitment to yourself to explore the worlds most beautiful and profound poetry.

Another important aspect of an actor's training is movement. At some point in a production, an actor has to move. An actor needs a flexible, fluid, yet strong and supple body. Perhaps the best movement techniques and exercises are those that combine flexibility with grace and poise. Classes in dance, Yoga, Tai Chi, and the study of the martial arts are all excellent avenues for actors to consider in the realm of movement training. Yoga may be one of the most perfect exercise systems ever developed. Yoga means "Union" - union of the body, mind, and spirit. The physical positions in Yoga - called the asanas - promote poise, grace, flexibility, strength, and agility. Yoga promotes relaxation, concentration, and a sense of balance. The slow and rhythmic motions of Yoga also develop grace and strength in a student. Classes in Yoga are offered at local schools, community colleges, and Yoga centers. The benefits of Yoga for an actor are immeasurable. Training in Yoga complements an actor's study of movement.   Studies in dance, fencing, karate, and any movement discipline can aid an actor immensely in training the instrument to its fullest potential.

Acting is an art, and like all art forms, the artist must continually practice honing his craft through constant practice and study. The actor must continue to grow and assimilate those techniques and skills that will promote artistic development. Acting is an art that uses the full spectrum of the human being - the full range of human emotions -

and it is essential that the actor perfect her instrument and imagination.

These, then, are some of the academic, professional, and commercial avenues of study. Learning is a lifelong process, and actors are no different from other professionals in staying abreast of the latest techniques. A life in the arts flourishes when an actor makes a commitment to constant self-improvement through training and education. Creativity is the key to an actor's ultimate success, and education is an essential component of such success. An instrument that is trained, honed, and focused is capable of rich imaginative impulses and creatively exciting choices.

CHAPTER FOUR
CABLE TELEVISION, VIDEO, AND THE ARTS

You could create your own TV show. Indeed, you could produce, write, and host a TV show on local cable television. As I mentioned in Chapter One, I created a TV show on the arts, entitled **"The Culture Corner,"** which aired Tuesdays at 8:30pm on a cable station in Pennsylvania. This television show on the arts was quite successful during its four years on the airwaves. What started as a TV show on the theatre arts soon became a showcase for all the arts - painting, sculpture, music, and dance to name but a few. The aspiration of this chapter is to take a specific look at just how you can go about creating your own TV program and realize the inherent rewards and challenges of cable TV.

Every cable provider must offer a community access station. This station airs programming geared toward community interest and events. Some stations are strictly noncommercial, and some provide advertising opportunities. The quality of productions produced by these stations may vary greatly depending on geography, population, and need. However, regardless of the available production values, hosting and/or producing your own cable program can be a rewarding, challenging, and enlightening experience. Local communities need a diversity of programming, and that's where you come in. If you can think of a television show that a local cable TV station might need or want, you can then approach them with your idea. Once your idea is accepted, then it's up to you as the producer of the show to find advertisers (since the local cable TV station will charge you for airtime and production costs). Once the cable TV station gives you the go-ahead for your show, the real work begins.

First, you'll want to get a copy of the demographic map of the station. This map can be used to show potential advertisers what the geographic range is - just how many households receive the cable station. You can use this map as a sales tool by showing potential advertisers the precise viewing area and audience. This is important information to any potential advertiser. During the four years that my TV show aired, I had a variety of sponsors advertise on the telecasts. Some of my advertisers included a tire company, a Realtor, a Tae Kwon Doe studio, an accountant, and an arts center.

Once you are armed with the appropriate information concerning population and demographics of the cable serving area, you'll want to write up a one- to two-page synopsis of your show. This synopsis will show the advertisers your vision, objectives, and intentions for the show. When you present the advertisers with your synopsis and geographic information you are clearly showing them the benefits of investing in and advertising on your cable TV show. When my cable TV show premiered in June 1991, I had only two advertisers. In May 1994 I was invited to do a telecast on the prestigious Philadelphia Antiques show. At that time, I had five advertisers, an arts grant from an Arts Center, and a handsome paycheck from a Philadelphia public relations firm for the telecast of this artistically important event. My show was featured in *Art Matters*, a prestigious arts magazine in the Philadelphia metropolitan area.

I later went on to produce a video about Hypnosis, and it was called, **"Hypnosis: The Key to Unlocking Your Mind's Power and Potential."** This hour-long video featured a respected hypnotherapist who shared the techniques of self–hypnosis in a clear, precise manner. Once again, I hosted, produced, and co-wrote the video. This video gave specific insights into eliminating such habits as smoking and overeating. This video was marketed to public libraries and individuals, and was sold in some local stores and bookstores. Also, it was offered in a national video catalogue. In each of these videos, I came up with the idea, contacted the appropriate professionals, and then wrote, hosted, and produced the video.

Recently, I hosted, co-wrote, and co-produced a video on Acupressure entitled, **"The Chinese Acupressure Facelift."** This video focuses on the acupressure techniques for a natural facelift. This video shows specific techniques for looking younger naturally through acupressure points on the face, head, and neck. A beautifully photographed video, "The Chinese Acupressure Facelift" is distributed nationally by a company from California, and is, without question, the most commercial of the videos that I have hosted. This video has the most beautiful production values of any video I have produced, and it is easy to see why it is distributed at a national level.

Creating videos then, is yet another possibility for aspiring actors and actresses. There is great creative autonomy in writing, hosting, and producing a video. Obviously, you need a director and editor to complete the project, so it is essential for you to contact local cable TV or video companies in your area. Creating your video is the first imaginative challenge, while marketing and distributing the video is your next challenge. Video distribution companies can be found on the Internet, or by perusing your local video store and reading the names of the distribution companies on the back of the videos. In any case, it is imperative that you create a distinctive product of great quality.

CHAPTER FIVE
TEACHING DRAMA

"Whenever you teach someone, you teach yourself as well," an adage goes, and this is particularly true in the realm of drama. Since actors and models experience periods of unemployment, you can take advantage of that reality by sharing your acting techniques, skills, and abilities through teaching drama to others. Teaching drama is a viable option for actors, and it can be an exciting alternative to conventional part-time jobs. You could create and conduct drama classes through art associations, community colleges, or even private seminars.

Many years ago, I created my own acting seminars, which I conducted privately. I charged $55 per student for a five-hour seminar. During the five hours, I taught acting techniques, voice, speech, movement, and improvisations. I would also cover the business aspect of the acting and modeling business. I placed ads in local newspapers and then rented a conference room at a local hotel.

The acting seminars gave me a great sense of artistic satisfaction since I was teaching something that I truly loved. If you consider teaching drama,

I'm sure you would find it rewarding.

The keys to success in the endeavor include having an authentic interest in teaching drama, having good ads that will catch the public's eye, and a clean comfortable space to conduct the acting seminar. Although it can be challenging to work with a variety of people of ages, degrees of talent, socioeconomic classes, and educational backgrounds, it can still be a successful experience if your intentions are pure and your enthusiasm is real. Once you've taken the ad out in a local paper, booked a conference room (it could be small depending on the size of your class), and prepared for the seminar, you're now ready to share your craft, your art, and your newly acquired acting skills.

THE ACTING SEMINAR

So what goes on in an acting seminar? How does one conduct a drama class? Well there are as many ways to approach this experience as is creatively imaginable. But, I've found several things that have worked for me over the years, so I'll share them with you. First and foremost, I have the students sit in whatever chairs they please, and encourage them to create a semicircle configuration (which is less formal) and introduce themselves. I attempt to create a low-key, subdued, friendly atmosphere. I ask the students about any prior performance experience.

After introductions are made, I take a few moments to present some of the theories of acting. In an attempt to define acting, I present my idea that "Acting is living truthfully, under the given circumstances, moment by moment." Although there are many fine definitions concerning the art of acting, I propose this idea to my class. It is essential to stress the truthfulness about acting and its "moment-to-moment" experience. Beginning acting students need to learn how to live in the moment if their acting is to possess an air of believability and credibility. Occasionally, I'll share a Zen story to illustrate the importance of living in the moment – the "eternal now" that Zen students and enthusiasts embrace.

Moment-to-moment acting is one of the first elements that students need to realize in a drama class. Once the definition of acting is proposed, it is time to put these ideas and ideals into practice. Improvisations are the perfect place to start for beginning students. Improvisations allow acting students to live truthfully under the given circumstances moment by moment. Improvisation acting allows creative freedom, focus, and insights into creating a scene.

IMPROVISATIONS

Here is an example of an improvisation that could be shared with an acting class. It requires three actors (perhaps two females and one male, or vice versa) and should help focus the actors on the task at hand. Here's the improv:

Two female friends are on vacation. It is a beautiful day in July, and they have been vacationing in New England. They are checking out of the Bed and Breakfast they have been staying in for the past three nights. Unfortunately, they don't realize that they have "maxed out" their credit cards and they are eighty dollars short for their bill. They are presented with a bill from the innkeeper, and the actors discover that they don't have enough money. They need to find the creative solution to this dilemma. The *obstacle* in the improv is the lack of money. The *objective* is to convince the innkeeper they can pay at a later date.

Improvs should always have an obstacle and an objective because they give the actors something to fight for and a place to go in the scene. There are numerous scenarios that can be achieved with improvisational acting. Once these are completed, it is time to introduce the students to scenes and scene work. It is also a good idea to videotape and play back the scenes at the end of the class so that the actors can see their work.

It's important to have a rich variety of scripts to assign the students. I use soap opera scripts, TV commercials, and contemporary comedies and dramas from films and TV. Modern classics from such American authors as Eugene O'Neill, Tennessee Williams, and Arthur Miller are perfect scripts for both novice and experienced actors to perform. You'll need a variety of two women scenes, two male scenes, and one male and one female scenes depending on the demographics of your class.

It's necessary to keep the acting class moving - that is flowing from one creative activity to another. It's essential to balance the activities; for instance, acting theories with improvisations; theatre games with scene work; and voice and speech work with movement exercises. As an acting teacher, you must be a "guide on the side" as well as a "sage on the stage." In a very real sense, an acting teacher is an artistic mid-wife, helping students to explore their creativity by breathing life into newly developed characters.

To summarize then, an acting seminar or class should include an introduction to acting, improvisations; voice and speech warm-ups; movement and stretching; and a wide variety of acting scenes from plays and TV/film scripts. The use of a TV and VCR to videotape scenes is useful, but not essential. It is important to keep the flow of the class and to keep the students focused on the creative activities. Yoga, tai chi, or modified ballet postures are also helpful for the movement part of the class. Acting classes and seminars can be creative, rewarding, and positive experiences for both the students and the teacher.

CHAPTER SIX
THE RESUME

As stated in the first chapter, an actor needs a good commercial headshot and resume. An actor's resume is vastly different from a conventional "real-world" resume. The actor's resume should include sections on theatre, video, TV, and film work. Include information on training, skills, and special abilities. Don't forget your physical statistics (height, weight, hair and eye color). It is essential that the resume be typed and easy to read. If you want your resume read and not tossed in the circular file, be clear, orderly, and concise. Agents, casting directors, and TV producers need things simple and easy.

If you are just starting out, no one expects you to have a lengthy resume. Every time you get an acting job, or make a local TV appearance, you should update your resume. Perhaps the easiest way to explain what goes where in an actors resume is to share my resume (see Appendix I). Resumes may have different styles and formats, but the sample presented is the format that has worked for me over the years.

Remember, the purpose of a resume is to show an actor's experience onstage or in front of the camera. Small successes can lead to greater successes. When I moved back north from Florida many years ago, I had only acted in two corporate videos and several TV commercials. Then, in a nine-month period, had several successful auditions, and appeared in twelve corporate videos in the Philadelphia, southern New Jersey, and Delaware area. My resume grew immensely, giving me more credits, greater confidence, and extensive experience in front of the camera. In fact, that year I acted in nine TV commercials, sixteen corporate videos, and literally dozens of modeling jobs. Each time I received a new credit, I immediately updated my resume. This is a shining example of what happened to me. It could indeed happen to you.

Consider making your resume as easy to read as possible. Make sure you keep unnecessary information off your resume, such as political affiliations, personal philosophy, astrological information, or anything that does not present you as a professional. You want your resume and headshot to appear as professional as possible; if you haven't had much work in TV or video, don't worry. Focus on the positive, and accentuate any work that you have completed and achieved in the theatre. A resume that highlights your strengths and experiences is imperative if you are to find work in the field of TV. Remember, local TV stations make infomercials as well as TV commercials.

Highlight any theatrical experiences you may have had in community theatre, dinner theatre, or regional theatre. Producers and casting directors respect stage work and quality public presentations. Eventually, someone will take a chance on you and cast you in that first TV commercial, infomercial, or corporate video. As a beginner, you need experience. If you have studied and worked in local or community theatre, highlight those experiences in your resume. Remember that there are many types and styles of resumes. Let's discuss another possibility for a resume.

THE BIOGRAPHICAL RESUME

This resume can also be reduced to a single page. And it helps if you have a digital photo of yourself to present on the top of your bio. First, you want to present your photo and name at the top of the paper. Then, you want to launch into your bio. The first paragraph of your resume should include any education and training. The second paragraph should state any theatre, TV, or video work that you have performed and accomplished. Once again, remember to keep your biographical resume succinct and to the point. Concentrate on your professional credits, training, education, and achievements.

A well-organized resume can get you work and help you grab the attention of those in power, who can put you in front of the camera. Yes, you can become a local TV celebrity, but it will take professionalism, patience, practice, and drive. If you believe this, then you can achieve it. Always put your most professional foot forward with a clean, clear, and specific resume. Your resume is your calling card to the world of TV, video, and film - make sure it is as professional and easy to read as possible. You want those in charge to see you in a professional light.

CHAPTER SEVEN
AGENTS

Ah, agents! You'll either love them, or hate them, or feel both love and disdain for them at the same time or at least some of the time. They can help your career or sabotage your career in the blink of an eye. However, you will eventually need an agent for some aspects of professional work. The process of getting an agent is not all that complicated. Once you have your headshot and resume, and have acquired some local work in community theatre, you are ready to approach an agent.

The safest way to find a reputable agent is to contact the SAG/AFTRA office in the largest city of your region or state. You'll want a SAG/AFTRA franchised agent, and you can easily get a list of agents in your state or local area from the Internet, the phone book, or a local SAG (Screen Actors Guild) office. You may want to consider passing on the agents who are affiliated with modeling schools. Agents affiliated with modeling schools will be more interested in selling you their (possibly costly) program than in actually getting you work. Now, this is not *always* the case, but you do have to approach these agencies with a wary eye. Yes, you need some training and experience, but you may not need it from their "special" commercial course that can possibly cost you hundreds of dollars. Do your homework and research. Once you've established that you are dealing with a professional and reputable agent, call them up. Ask practical questions. Inquire about their audition process, do exactly what they tell you, and above all behave in a professional manner.

WHAT HAPPENS AT AN AGENT'S INTERVIEW?

After you mail your headshot and resume to an agent in your area, you should follow up with a phone call in two or three weeks to see if they received your materials. If they have received your photo/resume and are interested in your "type," you may be invited in for an interview. Sometimes agents have specific days and times for interviewing new talent, (for example: Tuesdays from 1 to 3pm or Wednesdays from 2 to 4pm).

If an agent wishes to meet you, by all means make an effort to visit them in a timely manner. Once you arrive at the interview, remember that in the commercial world of acting and modeling, you are a "type." There is no sense fighting your "type" if you truly wish to work. I used to joke that I was paid as an actor and print model, "to impersonate a Republican." What I meant was that I projected the image of a young, professional, conservative businessman. In fact I was once told by a producer to "wear that exact blue-striped Italian suit to the TV commercial shoot." At the audition for that particular commercial, I thought they were impressed by my acting ability - now, in retrospect, I wonder if they were more impressed by my looks, my image, indeed, my very "type." Go with the flow. You can always prove to the world that you are a brilliant actor in your one-person show, or your production of *Hamlet*. You need to work, you need experience, and in life, the way you see yourself is not always the way the world sees you. Once again, go with the flow of your career.

It is important to become the best in your "type" that you can possibly be and project that image to the camera. Agents are necessary for some kinds of work, and you'll need to prove to them that you are professional and courteous in demeanor and attitude.

Reading copy is one of the things an agent will require you to do. Usually, the agent will have you read a brief TV commercial or corporate script. Make sure you ask questions about the characters objectives and intentions. Read the script slowly and silently at first. Then, if given the opportunity, read the script aloud in the hallway or in a corner of the room. When you return to the agent, you should be able to perform in a confident and relaxed manner. Acting in TV commercials can be fun. Make sure you relish this rich, creative opportunity.

Commercial acting can be an authentically enjoyable manner in which to make money and have a great professional time. Listen to the direction of the agent before commencing your reading. Make clear your creative choices when auditioning with your copy. Take your time. And of course have fun in a professional and creative manner. Once the audition is over and the agent releases you from the interview, make sure you thank them and quietly leave. It might take a few days to hear anything. Agents are busy people. After the meeting, remember to live your life, and continue your creative endeavors. If the agent doesn't select you, don't worry. Continue contacting agents in your geographic region. Something will break your way - it always does. However, it may not happen on your time schedule. Be patient. Work hard. Continue to improve. And keep auditioning for agents, directors, and producers. Also, have a dependable source of income. And, as to matters of work...read on!

CHAPTER EIGHT
SURVIVAL SKILLS

Alas, you'll need a job! Well, at the very least you'll need income in order to survive in our material world. Now, income can flow into your purse strings in any number of ways: meaningful work, financial investments, inheritance, and a job. The last one you'll probably hate the most. Income is income - all that counts is that it sustains and supports you, and that it is earned legally. Your bills are not going to go away, and they will never go away unless you win a multimillion-dollar lottery.

You will need to generate income while you commence your road to a local acting career. In fact, you'll need a dependable source of income while you pursue artistic ambitions and creative endeavors. This chapter is designed to help you discover the best survival skills for you in the realm of part-time or full-time jobs. Remember, you have to attend auditions to book some commercials and print ads. That means that many of these jobs are going to have hours that are different than the normal 9-to-5. Let's take a look at some possibilities that may suit you in your journey.

WAITING TABLES, BUSSING TABLES, OR HOST/HOSTESS

Pros: Working in a restaurant is one of the fastest ways to make money as an unskilled laborer. Although the hourly wage is often low, tips tend to offset this and produce handsome returns by the end of a shift. However, waiting tables can be hard physically, and quite stressful at times. In order to make the big bucks, you should be at a fine restaurant. The upside is that you can make good money in a short period of time. If you have a dinner shift, then you're open for auditions and working during the day. Most actors wait tables at some point in their careers. It is perhaps the biggest cliché for actors and the most lucrative experience while waiting for their big break.

Cons: Waiting tables is very hard. It can exhaust you physically, mentally, and emotionally. It is one of the most stressful jobs that you can have, and it does require some degree of skill. If you stress easily, you may want to rethink waiting tables as an alternative career. Waiting tables can be difficult, demeaning, and yes even demanding work. It can sap your energies. All in all, it's a young person's game. Keep looking, and you can find more meaningful work.

TEACHER OR SUBSTITUTE TEACHER

Pros: If you have a degree in education, or live in a state where teachers are desperately needed and the state issues emergency certificates, you could consider teaching as an alternative. You should have an authentic interest in teaching and communicating your knowledge. And, teaching can be a well-paid experience these days. Substitute teaching requires a little commitment for the long term, and could fit into your schedule for auditions and work. I once held a part-time gifted education job, with hours of Monday through Friday, 8am-12:15pm. In the afternoons I would act in TV commercials or corporate videos in Philadelphia or Harrisburg. It can be done. I am proof of this. At times, it was the best of both worlds, teaching in the morning, acting in the afternoon.

Cons: One of the problems with teaching is that it can tie you up for a full day's shoot or audition in the morning. A full-time teaching job makes it difficult to go off and do print ads, TV commercials or videos. A teaching job can cost you auditions and work unless you take personal or sick days. Substitute teaching can be one of the most wretched experiences ever devised - it's "Les Miserables." Some of the worst days in my life were days spent substitute teaching. Kindergarten is fine, but if you are substituting in junior high, you can guarantee that the kids will be rude, ill mannered, and at the very least, challenge everything that comes out of your mouth. I don't mean to offend any parents here, but unless you have a strong stomach, try something else. Also, the money is usually so-so. I'll pass.

TELEMARKETING

Pros: You get to call people up and bother them. You get to interrupt people, just as they're sitting down to dinner, and ask them a slew of questions about garden hoses, or why they haven't paid their credit card bills on time. And you get paid for this. Shifts can be part-time or full-time. The pay varies, and bonuses are possible. It can be boring, grueling, and mentally exhausting.

Cons: Same as the pros. See above.

SALES

Pros: A position in sales, as a representative for a company, may be one avenue for aspiring actors to explore. A career in real estate sales, for instance, gives a performer enough flexible and free time to audition and work occasionally in commercials or print. My wife Debra was a Realtor for several years, and she had extreme flexibility in her schedule. Real estate sales people can often "make their own of hours." Thus, a position in real estate sales, or some form of sales that allows flexibility in the schedule may quite possibly be the best alternative for an aspiring local actor.

Cons: The biggest problem with real estate sales is that most offices do not pay a salary. Realtors almost always work strictly on commission. There are, of course, exceptions. However, full-time real estate sales will prove to be unpredictable and scary. You can lose thousands of dollars on one phone call. But if you have talent and enough drive you can do extremely well. However, you will be at the beck and call of clients, and often find yourself working evenings and weekends. There are other sales jobs out there, but most have set hours, just like other jobs.

Just remember that most of you will need a job that gives you a steady, dependable paycheck, and allows flexibility and free time. You **gotta** make a living.

CHAPTER NINE
PUTTING IT ALL TOGETHER

One of the most important things in life is to take knowledge and techniques and put them into practical action. The ultimate goal of this book is to help local actors find a successful creative outlet for their talents. It takes time and training to achieve purposeful goals. You must have a sense of commitment and a strong dose of ambition to make things happen. Stick to your goals and you can achieve your dreams. Dedication, hard work, and persistence pay off when pursuing any substantial life goal.

Another important avenue for aspiring actors to consider is to become involved with art associations. Over the years I have taught at two of the finest art associations on the East Coast - the Ocean City Arts Center in Ocean City New Jersey, and the Community School of Music and the Arts in Reading, Pennsylvania.

Both associations offer a wide variety of classes in the arts. Each Association is well managed and well organized, providing their respective communities with active programs and events that enhance the cultural life of their region.

Mr. Cedric Elmer guided the Community School of Music and the Arts in Reading, Pennsylvania for many years. Under his excellent leadership and guidance this unique arts school contributed creatively to the community. Mr. Elmer provided that kind of artistic vision and leadership that made the community school a vital, vibrant, and significant artistic institution in its geographic area. The Ocean City Arts Center also offers a diversified selection of artistic course offerings. Located in a beautiful community building in the family friendly seaside resort of Ocean City, New Jersey, the Arts Center is an important force in its cultural community.

It was an authentic pleasure to teach drama at these artistic institutions. Both institutions provide teachers and students with a clean, comfortable, and safe environment for teachers and students. Both institutions are committed to providing the finest art courses with well-trained and well-educated teachers. If teaching drama is important to you, it's essential to find an art association that provides the opportunities that these associations offer.

Another important aspect to acting locally is exploring local community events that will put your name and face before the public. Local cable TV shows need hosts for local TV events such as parades, special events, and community days. Get involved with local television. Get out there. Make sure you explore all the avenues of local mass communication, radio, TV, newspaper, and community theatre. Crucial to your quest for success will be an understanding of public relations. It's essential that you explore every avenue of public relations that is available to you in order to promote yourself and your talents. No matter what your age, social and economic background, formal education, or training, you can make the difference in your career through dedication and focused hard work.

Too many beginners don't understand that in order to achieve your goals, you must work hard in order to become successful. Know how to apply yourself. Show business is one of the most difficult businesses to break into and just because you're trying to break into it in your own hometown, doesn't mean it will be a walk in the park. Don't forget that just about everybody wants to be in show business. Take a look at how many **reality television** shows there are on the air right now. Regardless of all the hard work it will take for you to accomplish many of your dreams in this business, the rewards can be huge. Not just financially, but creatively, physically, and emotionally.

Throughout this book I use the term professional and professionalism frequently. It occurs to me that you may not know exactly what I mean. So I have come up with a list that I affectionately term The Ten Commandments of Professionalism and they are as follows:

1. Always arrive at least 15 minutes early for every job, audition, or meeting.

2. Be observant and courteous. Never swear or waste other people's time.

3. Never criticize the project or copy you are reading.

4. Always come prepared. Know your lines when appropriate and bring proper clothing and makeup.

5. Always say thank you after each audition, job, or meeting. Sometimes a thank you note is a nice touch.

6. Stay focused and alert at every job. Be prepared to wait. Be prepared to start.

7. Treat everyone on the set with respect, regardless of his or her job title.

8. Keep political and religious opinions to yourself.

9. Approach every audition, job, or meeting with enthusiasm and passion for the work. Love what you do and show it.

10. Be kind and considerate, and treat others the way you want to be treated.

So there you have it, a few simple rules to help you illuminate a professional appearance. If you can keep these principles in mind and practice at least half of them regularly, you'll stand out and people will want to work with you.

Remember to make contact with people who can influence your career, and get involved in as many local media events as possible. Keep true to your dreams and remember Goethe's great words, "Whatever you do, or think you can do, begin it. Genius has magic, power, and boldness in it. Begin it now."

APPENDIX 1
TERRY HARRIS

Height: 5'11"
Weight: 185 Lbs.
Eyes: Blue
Hair: Light
Brown

TELEVISION
Co-Producer, writer, and host of *The Chinese Acupressure Facelift*
Producer, Creator, Writer and actor for *Wavelength,* a Children's Television Show
Host and Producer *The Culture Corner,* PCTV
Host, "The Rebuilding of a Smile," WFMZ-TV
Reporter/Producer, "Time Out!" Twin County Cable TV 4
Co-Host, "Pretty Pickin's Jewelry Showcase," PCTV
Host, *The Renaissance Series,* an educational video series on the arts

STAGE

Romeo and Juliet Manatee Theatre	-Romeo
Born Yesterday Island Theatre	-Paul Verrall
Merlin!	-Young King Arthur -Old King Vortiger

Asolo Theatre
Ah, Wilderness!   -Richard Miller
Vasey Theatre
Troilus and Cressida   -Aneas
Villanova University
Once in a Wilde   -Vyvyan
Philadelphia Theatre Co.
Between Now and Then -Jonathan
Philadelphia Theatre Co.
The Taming of the Shrew -Lucentio
Philadelphia Theatre Co.
The Shadow Box   -Steve
Asolo Theatre
A History of the American Film-Eric
Asolo Theatre
Hunger and Bread   -Eugene
Philadelphia Theatre Co.
The Rimers of Eldritch   -Walter
Players Studio One
The Tempest   -Sebasitan
SKAT Theatre
Come Back to the Five and Dime,
Jimmie Dean, Jimmie Dean -Joe
SKAT Theatre

(Please note that the name of the theatre company should be on the same line as the Play and character.)

VIDEO

SMS, medical training video, SHOOTERS production

Grolier Encyclopedia Inc., educational training video

Chester County Condominium, promotional video

Lakeside West Resort, promotional video

Devereux Foundation, training video

Faulkner Pontiac, training video

First National Bank, corporate image video

Donnelley Directory, industrial training video

General Motors, industrial training video

Exide Corporation, training video

Parke Davis Pharmaceuticals, medical training video

DuPont Company, "Creative Health Package," sales promotional video

Mitsubishi Corporation, industrial training video

DuPont Company, "EMP," training video

The Lighthouse Drug Rehabilitation, medical training video

DuPont Company, "Sales Incentive Compensation Program," training video

McNeil Pharmaceuticals, training video

DuPont Company, "Prepmaster," training video

Ravensburger, "Games and Puzzles," international training video

COMMERCIALS

List available upon request

TRAINING
Master of Arts in Theatre - Villanova University
Master of Fine Arts in Acting Program - The Asolo
State Theatre
BA in Theatre/Communications - Villanova
University
The Weist-Barron School of Television Acting, New
York

WORKSHOPS
Lisa Mionie, Viacom Productions
Los Angeles, Film Acting Seminar
Irene Baird, Acting in Shakespeare Seminar
Lon Winston, Performance Theory Workshop
Tony Barr, Acting for the Camera Workshop
Mari Lyn Henry, TV and Film Acting Seminar

APPENDIX II
TERRY HARRIS

Terry Harris has had extensive experience in theatre, TV, and communications, and holds a **Master of Arts** degree in Theatre, a **Bachelor of Arts** degree in Communications, and a **Bachelor of Science** degree in Education from **Villanova University**. He did extensive graduate work in theatre at the Master of Fine Arts in Acting program at Florida State University in conjunction with the **Asolo State Theatre**. Mr. Harris also did intensive graduate work in **Gifted Education** at **Nova University**. Prior to his University education, he was educated at Chestnut Hill Academy, Methacton High School, Plymouth Meeting Friends School, and the Holland School.

Terry Harris is the host, writer, and producer of *The Renaissance Series*, an educational video series on the arts. He is also the host, co–writer, and co–producer of *The Chinese Acupressure Facelift* video. Terry has hosted such television shows as *The Rebuilding of a Smile* for WFMZ TV, and *The Culture Corner* – a television show devoted to the arts for PCTV. He is also the host, producer, and co–writer of the video, *Hypnosis: The Key to Unlocking Your Mind's Power and Potential*. He is the creator, writer, and producer of

Wavelength, a children's educational television show. The pilot show was produced in conjunction with Time Warner Cable of Reading, Pennsylvania.

As an actor, Terry Harris has appeared in over 50 TV commercials, including several as the spokesperson for **New Frontier** magazine. He has performed in over 30 plays, 35 corporate videos, and over 250 print ads, including a national print ad for Century 21 Home Improvements. In 1998 and 1999, he appeared in a major print-modeling ad for Pennsylvania Insurance Fraud. His commercial print-modeling work includes magazine ads, newspaper ads, billboards, and brochures. He has acted with the Philadelphia Theatre Company and The Villanova Summer Shakespeare Festival.

As an educator, Terry Harris has taught Gifted Education, Theatre, English, and Speech at a variety of educational levels. He has served as the Gifted Coordinator for Secondary Education at Wilson School District in Pennsylvania, and taught Theatre and Integrative Arts at **Penn State University** from 1994 to 1998. Terry has also written such books as *The Loneliest Leprechaun, Resplendent Rainbow, How to Get an Acting Job Outside of New York and Hollywood, Developing Your Child's CQ,* and a collection of poetry entitled *Cape May, My Love.*